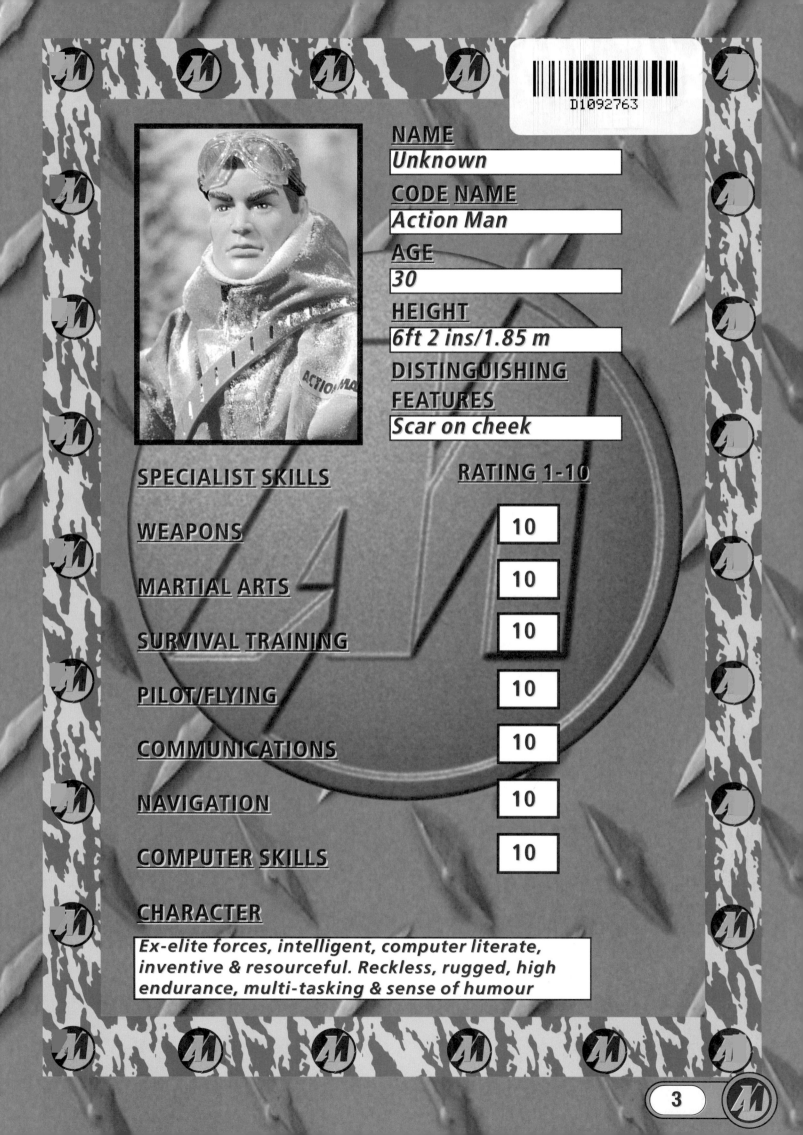

NAME
Unknown

CODE NAME
Action Man

AGE
30

HEIGHT
6ft 2 ins/1.85 m

DISTINGUISHING FEATURES
Scar on cheek

SPECIALIST SKILLS

RATING 1-10

WEAPONS — 10

MARTIAL ARTS — 10

SURVIVAL TRAINING — 10

PILOT/FLYING — 10

COMMUNICATIONS — 10

NAVIGATION — 10

COMPUTER SKILLS — 10

CHARACTER

Ex-elite forces, intelligent, computer literate, inventive & resourceful. Reckless, rugged, high endurance, multi-tasking & sense of humour

D1092763

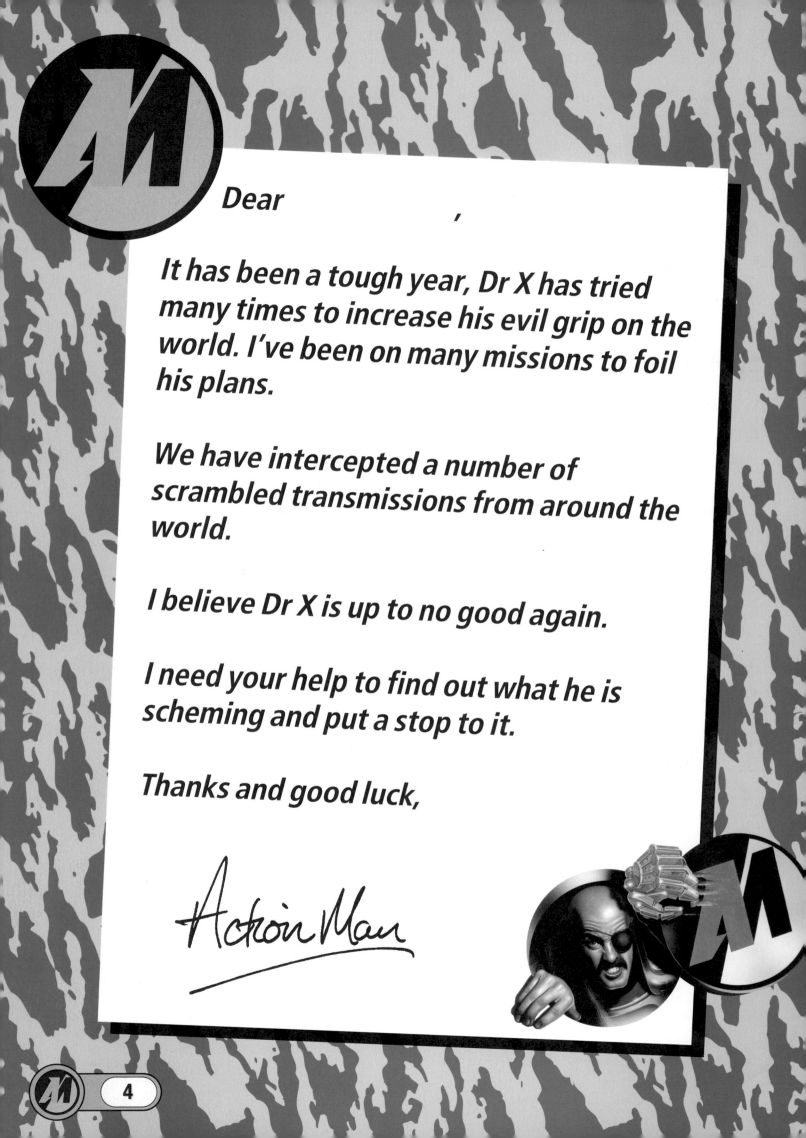

Dear   ,

It has been a tough year, Dr X has tried many times to increase his evil grip on the world. I've been on many missions to foil his plans.

We have intercepted a number of scrambled transmissions from around the world.

I believe Dr X is up to no good again.

I need your help to find out what he is scheming and put a stop to it.

Thanks and good luck,

Action Man

MISSION CONTENTS

Action Man annual is published
by
Pedigree Books
The Old Rectory
Matford Lane
Exeter EX2 4PS

© Hasbro International Inc.
Licensed by 3D Licensing Ltd.

PROFILE: DR X

NAME
UNKNOWN
ALIAS
DR X
AGE
30
HEIGHT
6ft 2 ins/1.85 m
DISTINGUISHING FEATURES
CYBERNETIC EYE & HAND, X TATOO ON CHEST,

MESSAGE INTERCEPT: from Dr X...

"Look at the map of the world. It is a series of high points and low points. Through out the history of the human race it has always been that he who takes the high ground wins the battle. I, Dr X, master of evil will take that high ground and defeat my foes, especially that crawling insect who goes by the absurd name of Action Man. I will show him more action than he dreams of in his worst nightmares for I am Dr X master of chaos.
Join with me. Climb with me. Let me give you the world..."

PSYCHOLOGICAL PROFILE
Psychopathic, no respect for human life, highly intelligent, if he can't beat you he'll eat you.

AREA OF OPERATIONS

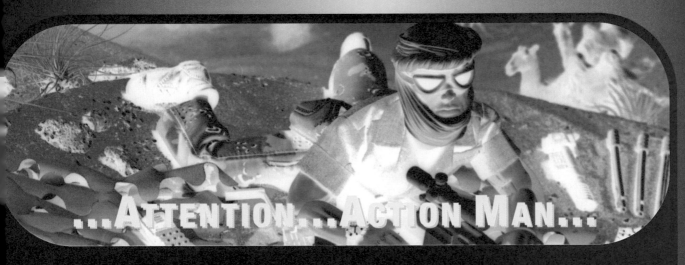

...ATTENTION...ACTION MAN...

Message:
Illegal weapons shipments are leaving Russia via desert region in the East of the country...we believe terrorists have arranged a meeting with their arms suppliers in 36 hours...

Cause:
Break up of old Soviet Union has seen huge rise in crime with many members of the armed forces exchanging their weapons for money or drugs...

Threat:
Splinter groups are gaining access to fearsome weapons and this is a major danger to world peace...

Mission:
Intercept weapons suppliers at exchange point and identify both them and the buyers...Neutralise if opportunity presents itself...

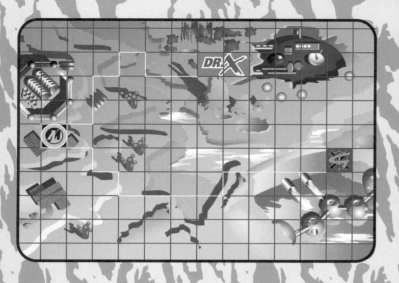

target area

Northern reaches of Gobi Desert...

threat assessment

Encampment containing around 180 terrorists...

language

Sub-Mongolian dialect...

potential hazards

Scorpion stings to Stinger Missiles!...

Desert Information

population

sparse, traditionally nomadic tribesmen

temperature

blazing hot by day, bitterly cold by night, the desert is one of the most inhospitable places known to man. Deserts like The Sahara in Africa can reach more than 50C in the day while the Gobi, which sits in Mongolia and Russia can be as cold as -20C in winter.

climate

The true definition of a desert is , however, its lack of water, with less than 25 cm of rain a year.

flora and fauna

Plants and animals do survive, adapted to the harsh conditions to need little water and having the ability to lie dormant for long periods. Cactus, palm trees, camels, snakes, scorpions, rats

desert patrol

- desert uniform
- camouflage net
- mobile phone
- machine pistol
- water bottle
- goggles
- flares
- assault rifle
- slr camera
- grenades

- bullet proof screen
- armour plated shell
- SAM missiles
- titanium roll cage
- all terrain tyres
- **4x4 turbo**

Before every mission Action Man has to choose exactly the right equipment for the terrrain and conditions he will be in.

Now you must help him decide what to use based on what you know about deserts. Use the boxes to tick the equipment you have selected.

desert uniform ✓	4x4 Jeep ✓	grenades ✓
camouflage net ✓	rollerblades ☐	slr camera ✓
mobile phone ✓	gyrocopter ☐	flares ☐
machine pistol ✓	machine gun ✓	goggles ✓
water bottle ✓	stealth jet ☐	chocolate ✓

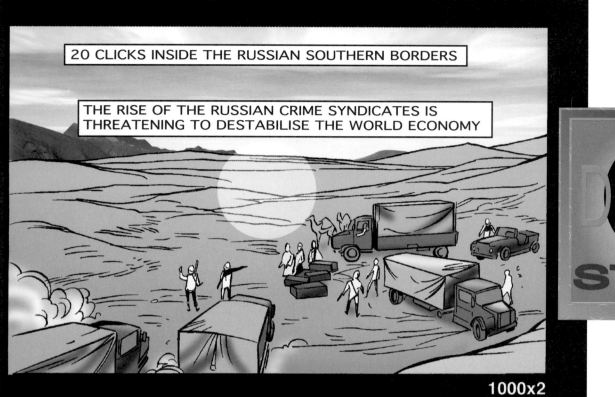

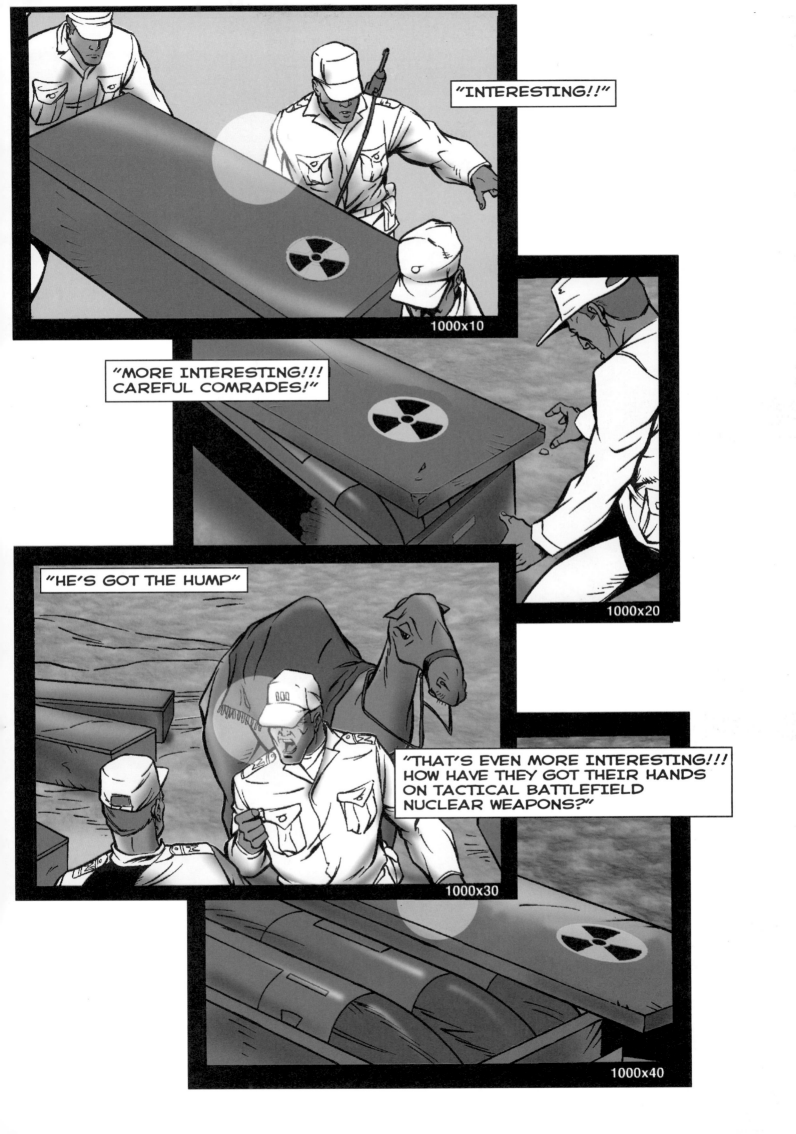

Action Man needs to debrief the European Defence Agency. Can you help him extract the key information from the mission he has just completed.

Answer the questions below by ticking the correct solution in the box provided.

what type of weapons have gone missing?	chemical	✓	nuclear	✓	biological	✓
which regiment are the soldiers from?	black sea kommandos	✓	black paratroopers	✓	sea marines	✓
who commands the soldiers?	captain yeltski	✓	admiral stavi	✓	general zil	✓
what tanks were attacking Action Man?	T 55	✓	T60	✓	T21	✓
which agency does Action Man need to call?	CIA	✓	EDA	✓	MI5	✓

Answers can be found on page 30

Answers from page 29:

what type of weapons have gone missing?	*nuclear*
which regiment are the soldiers from?	*black sea kommandos*
who commands the soldiers?	*general zil*
what tanks were attacking Action Man?	*T55*
which agency does Action Man need to call?	*EDA*

Design a new piece of equipment for Action Man to use in the desert and when you have done it paste it into this box.

AREA OF OPERATIONS

...ATTENTION...ACTION MAN...

Message:
A warehouse has been located on the outskirts of Moscow linked to the Russian Mafia - the Kosa Nostrovya - ...there may be possible links between this group and General Zil...

Cause:
We believe that this may be a base from which they may be planning an as-yet unknown criminal enterprise...

Threat:
Kosa Nostrovya gangs heavily armed and notoriously ruthless...

Mission:
Locate and investigate warehouse, report back to the EDA, find out who is behind these incidents...

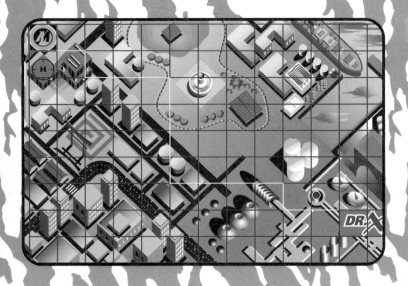

target area

Outer limits of Moscow...

threat assessment

Unknown number of Russian Kosa Nostrovya...

language

Russian...

potential hazards

Kosa Nostrovya, Russian Renegade troops...

Urban Information

population

Moscow is the largest city in Europe. Russia is the largest country in the world.

temperature

The temperature ranges from 25C to 30 C in summer to little as - 20C in winter.

climate

In winter capital can get heavy snow falls, which can cause problems with driving around.

recent history

In recent times there have been two coups (illegally trying to overthrow the government). The first was the failed attempt to overthrow President Gorbachev in 1991, the second in 1993 against President Yeltsin which also failed.

The Kosa Nostrovya is the name given to the Russian Mafia.

Mission data: Equipment

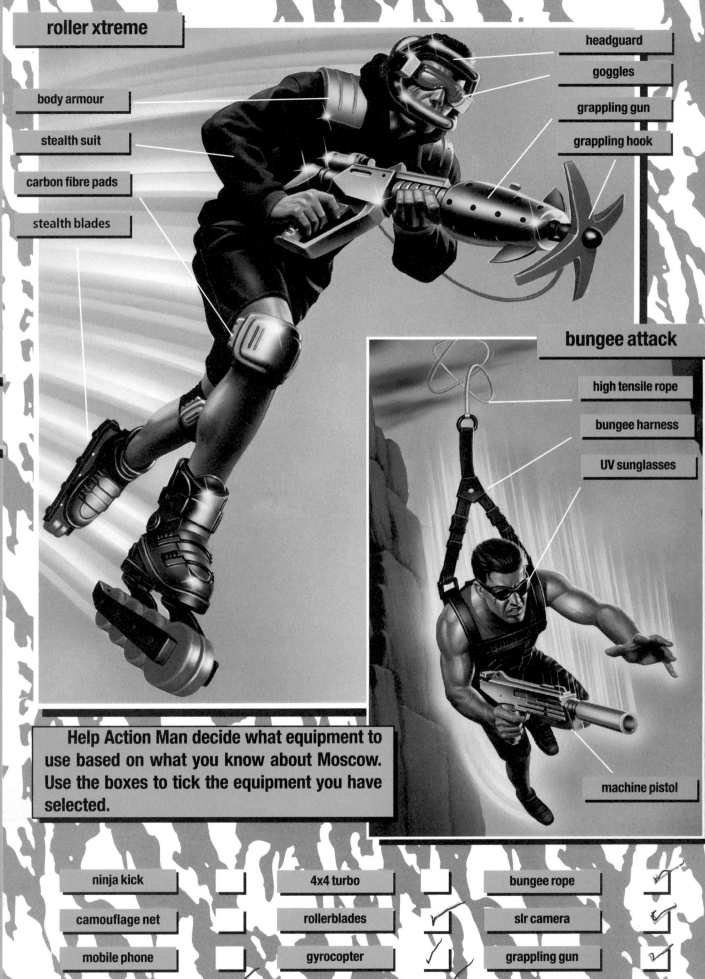

roller xtreme

headguard

goggles

grappling gun

grappling hook

body armour

stealth suit

carbon fibre pads

stealth blades

bungee attack

high tensile rope

bungee harness

UV sunglasses

machine pistol

Help Action Man decide what equipment to use based on what you know about Moscow. Use the boxes to tick the equipment you have selected.

ninja kick		4x4 turbo		bungee rope	✓
camouflage net		rollerblades	✓	slr camera	✓
mobile phone		gyrocopter	✓	grappling gun	✓
machine pistol	✓	grappling hook	✓	UV sunglasses	✓
water bottle	✓	stealth jet		Super Bike	✓

PROFILE: GENERAL ZIL

Name: General Askoda Zil
Nickname: Skipski
Age: 43
Profile: Cruelly ambitious, coldly
calculating, merciless
Links: Zitron Xantya, boss of
Russian Mafia outfit,
the Kosa Nostrovya.
Report: Joint property company
purchasing large amounts
of property on high ground...
London, San Francisco, Paris,
Tokyo... Large warehouse
on outskirts of Moscow...

"TO RUSSIA WITH LOVE"

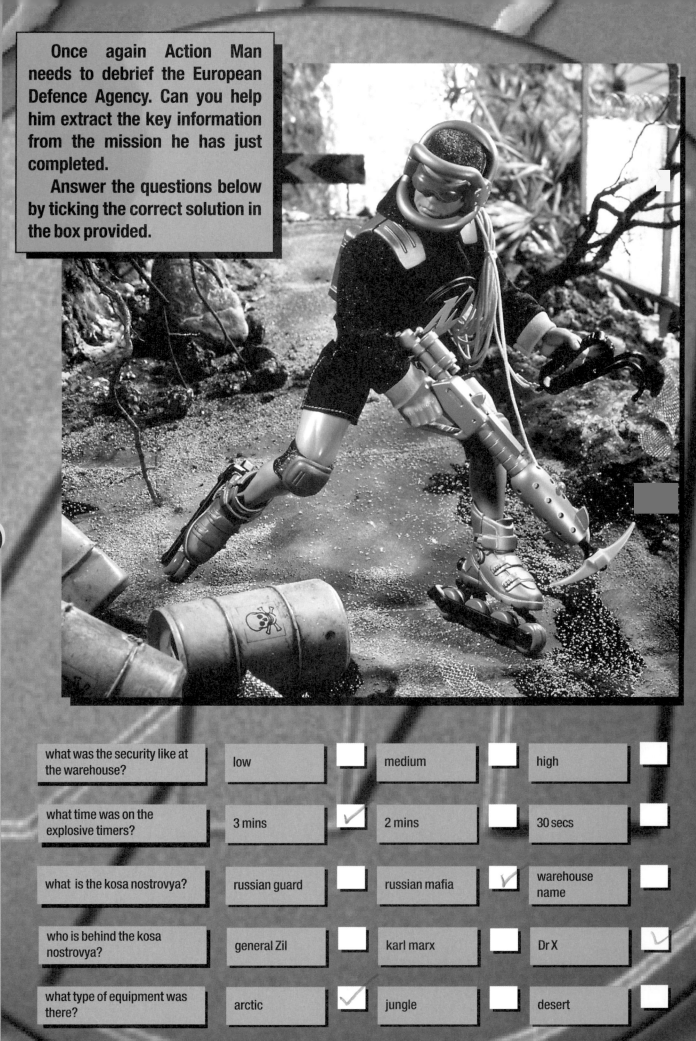

Once again Action Man needs to debrief the European Defence Agency. Can you help him extract the key information from the mission he has just completed.

Answer the questions below by ticking the correct solution in the box provided.

what was the security like at the warehouse?	low	☐	medium	☐	high	☐
what time was on the explosive timers?	3 mins	✓	2 mins	☐	30 secs	☐
what is the kosa nostrovya?	russian guard	☐	russian mafia	✓	warehouse name	☐
who is behind the kosa nostrovya?	general Zil	☐	karl marx	☐	Dr X	✓
what type of equipment was there?	arctic	✓	jungle	☐	desert	☐

Answers can be found on page 56

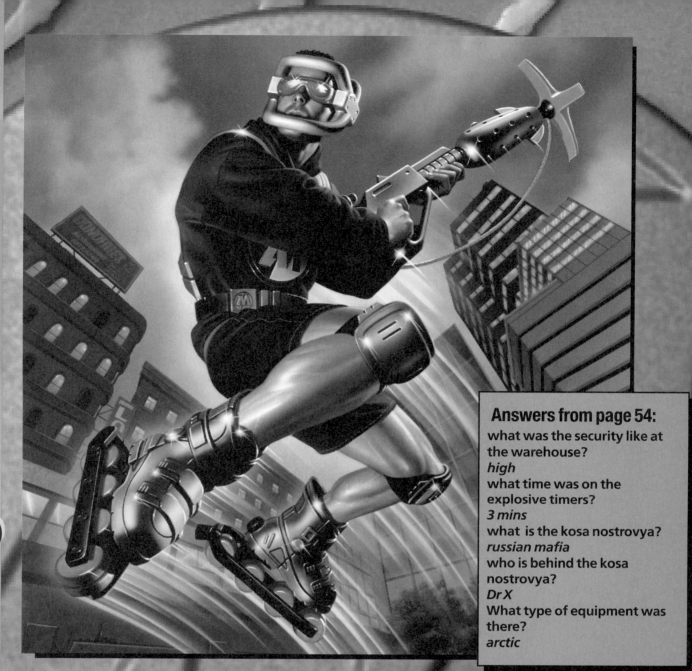

Answers from page 54:
what was the security like at the warehouse?
high
what time was on the explosive timers?
3 mins
what is the kosa nostrovya?
russian mafia
who is behind the kosa nostrovya?
Dr X
What type of equipment was there?
arctic

Design a new piece of equipment for Action Man to use with his Roller Blades

AREA OF OPERATIONS

...ATTENTION...ACTION MAN...

Message:
We have information that General Zil has a dacha - holiday house -
in the Siberian forests...He has been reported to have been seen
on route....

Cause:
We believe that he may be meeting his co-conspirators and
planning a major criminal act that could affect the whole world....

Threat:
Russian Black Sea Kommandos loyal to General Zil...these are
some of their elite forces...

Mission:
To locate the dacha...gain access and report back as to what
General Zil is planning... apprehend if possible...

target area

Siberian Forest...General Zil's Dacha

threat assessment

unknown number of Black Sea Kommandos...

language

Russian, Siberian Accent...

potential hazards

Mines, trip wires, electronic security...

Forest Information

population

sparse, traditionally timber workers

temperature

The Siberian Forests are huge, some of the largest in the world. the temperatures range from 15C in the summer to -40C in the winters.

climate

Siberia has large snow falls in winter and can be humid in summer in the southern parts.

flora and fauna

The forests are made up of coniferous forests, otherwise known as evergreen forests. The shape of many evergreen trees enables the snow to slide off their branches. There are many types of animals in the forest, some of which are dangerous, such as wolves, bears and, very rare, Siberian tigers.

Mission data: Equipment

gyrocopter
anti -glare visor
turbo jet engine
heavy body armour
missiles
machine pistol
data screen
carbon fibre body
night search light
missiles

stun gas arrows
carbon gauntlets
combat jacket
composite bow
counter weights
bowman

Decide what equipment to use based on what you know about forests. Use the boxes to tick the equipment you have selected.

stun gas arrows	✓	bungee rope		grenades	✓
carbon gauntlets		rollerblades		heavy body armour	✓
mobile phone		gyrocopter		flares	✓
machine pistol	✓	machine gun	✓	anti-glare visor	✓
water bottle		stealth jet		composite bow	

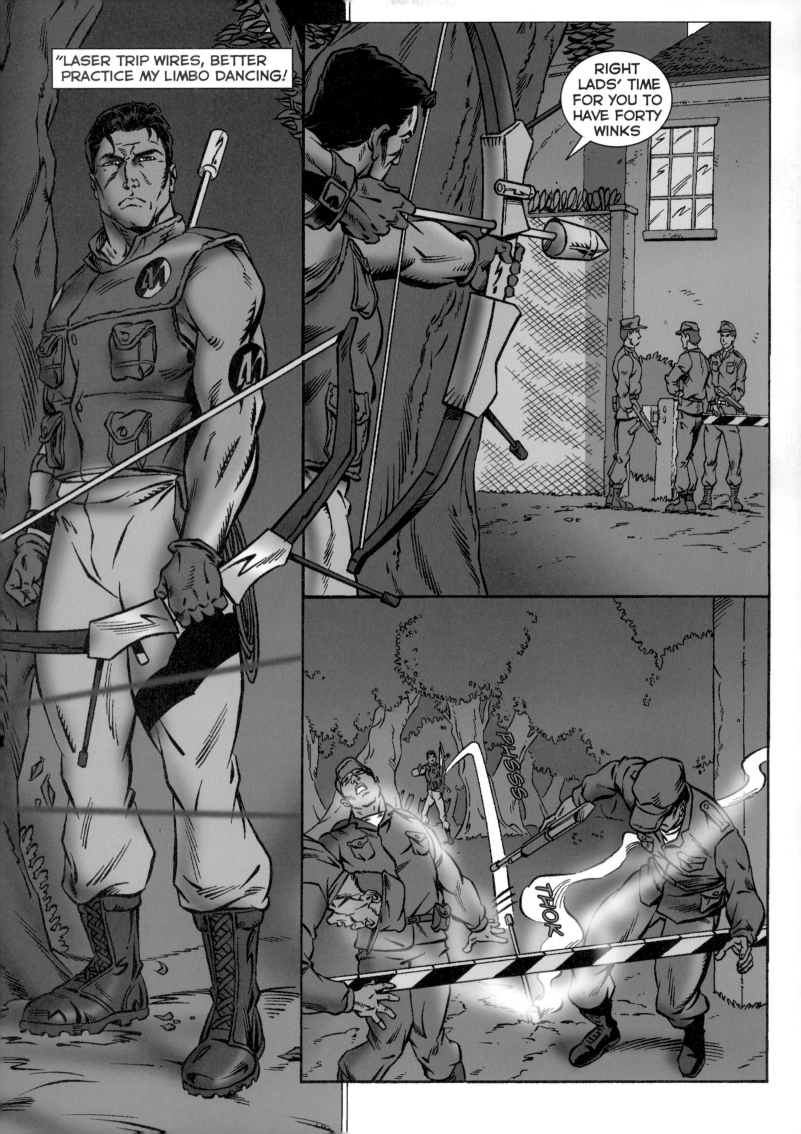

Debrief the European Defence Agency. Can you help extract the key information from the mission Action Man has just completed.

Answer the questions below by ticking the correct solution in the box provided.

what is a dacha?	defensive mound	☐	holiday house	✓	secret weapon	☐
who is General Zil meeting?	russia's president	☐	action man	☐	Dr X	✓
what is the is their evil plan?	flood the earth	✓	blow up the world	☐	freeze the planet	☐
what weapons are they going to use?	chemical	☐	nuclear	✓	biological	☐
where have the weapons been sent?	europe	☐	south pole	☐	arctic ice cap	✓

Answers can be found on page 80

79

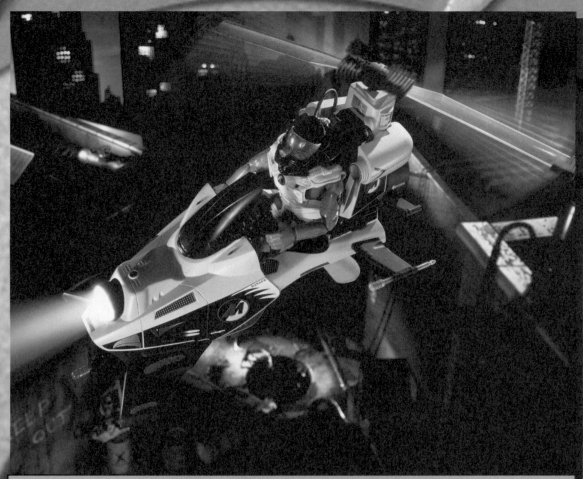

Answers from page 79:

what is a dacha?	*holiday house*
who is General Zil meeting with?	*Dr X*
what is the evil plan?	*flood the earth*
what weapon are they going to use?	*nuclear*
where have the weapons been sent?	*arctic Ice cap*

Design a new piece of equipment for Action Man to use in the forest and when you have done it paste it into this box.

AREA OF OPERATIONS

...ATTENTION...ACTION MAN...

Message:
Satellite photos have identified a base on the polar ice cap...

Cause:
We believe that this is Dr X's command and control centre where he will set off his nuclear weapons...

Threat:
Dr X's ruthless thugs and possible Black Sea Kommandos that may have escaped with him...

Mission:
To infiltrate Dr X's ice station without being detected...disable the nuclear weapons...and apprehend Dr X...

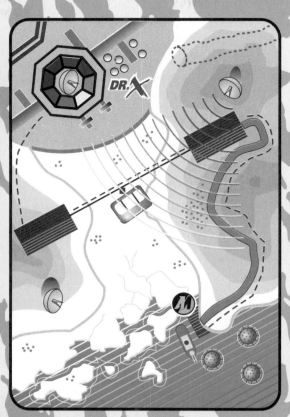

target area

Polar ice cap

threat assessment

Dr X's thugs...unknown number of Black Sea Kommandos

language

Inuit...

potential hazards

freezing temperatures...electronic security measures...rogue polar bears...killer whales in the sea

Arctic Information

population

Some Inuit Indians venture to the edge of the main ice pack. The Arctic also has many scientific stations and military bases

temperature

There are freezing temperatures all year round. The normal range is - 10 C to over - 50C

climate

The polar regions are probably the most inhospitable places on earth, alongside the Sahara desert. In the summer it is light all day, and in the winter it is dark all day. Some snow storms can last for days.

flora and fauna

There are no plants on the Arctic ice cap itself, though there are some plants in Antarctica. As far as animal life goes, there are polar bears, harp seals, bearded and hooded seals.

arctic sledge

survival clothing

missile

satellite radar pack

range finder lens

assault rifle

tracker collar

command centre

carbon fibre ice sled

arctic diver

navy seal torches

ice drill

Help Action Man decide what equipment to use based on what you know about the Arctic. Use the boxes to tick the equipment you have selected.

arctic dry suit

ninja kick		survival clothing		bungee rope	
camouflage net		navy seal torches		slr camera	
mobile phone		gyrocopter		grappling gun	
machine pistol		grappling hook		ice drill	
arctic dry suit		stealth jet		carbon fibre ice sled	

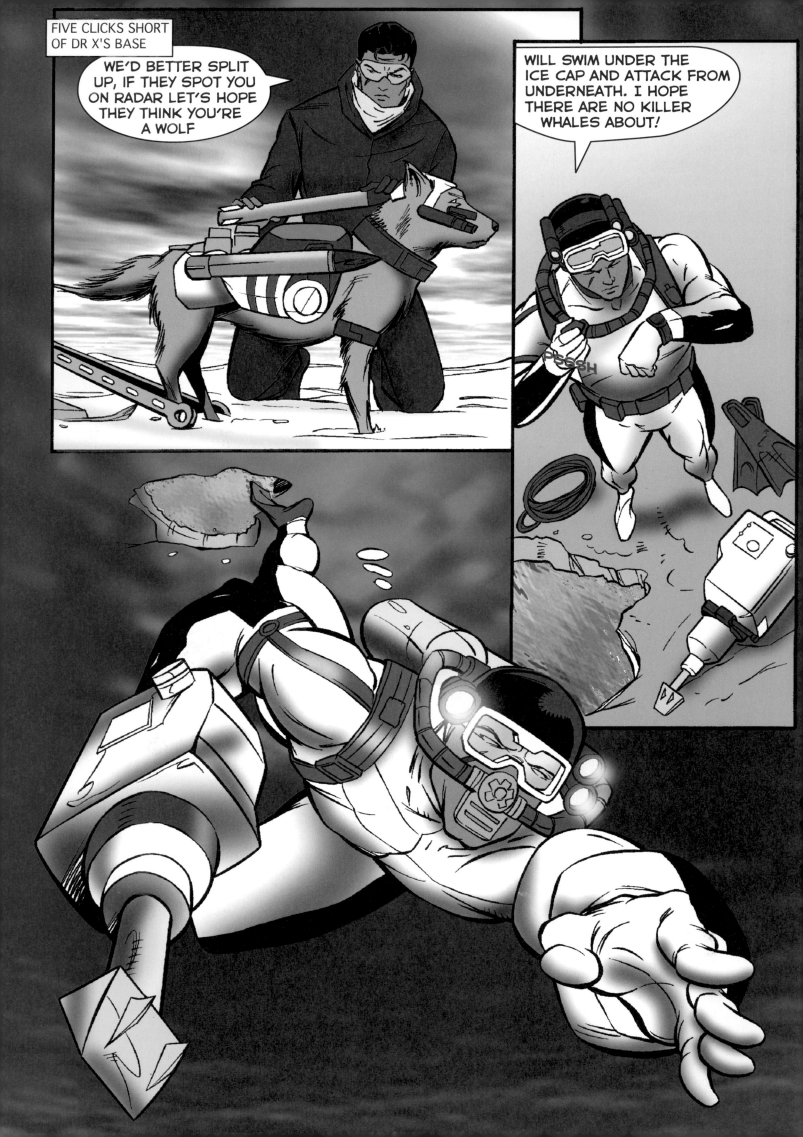

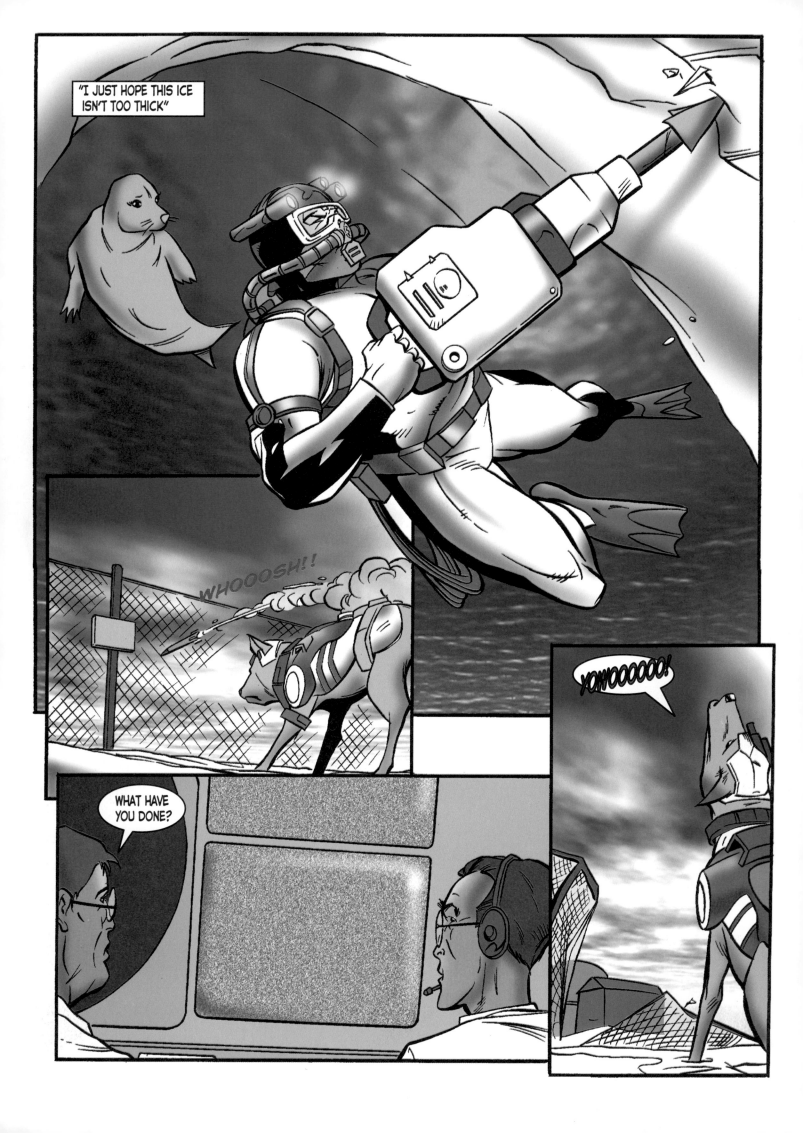

SCRIPT: SAM ANDREWS
PENCILS: W!LDMAN
INKS: GRIFFITHS
GEORGIOU
& BASKERVILLE
COLOURS: W!LDMAN
WITH ASSISTS FROM:
LESLEY AND FRANK

Debrief the European Defence Agency for the final time. Can you help Action Man extract the key information from the mission he has just completed.

Answer the questions below by ticking the correct solution in the box provided.

how far out does Action Man land?	20 klicks	☒	50 klicks	✓	10 klicks	☒
what is the name of Action Man's dog?	rufus	☒	K- 9	☒	blizzard	✓
how does Action Man get into the base?	under the ice	✓	over the fence	☒	through the gates	☒
how long does Dr X set the count down for?	5 hours	☒	1 hour	☒	30 minutes	✓
how many seconds are left when it is stopped?	10 seconds	☒	2 seconds	✓	30 seconds	☒

Answers can be found on page 106

Answers from page 104:

how far out does Action Man land?
50 klicks
what is the name of Action Man's dog?
blizzard
how does Action Man get into the base?
under the ice
how long does Dr X set the count down for?
30 minutes
how many seconds are left when it is stopped?
2 seconds

Design a new piece of equipment for Action Man to use in the Arctic

....message from Action Man

Thanks for your help in what has been my toughest set of missions to date.

Without your assistance I would not have been able to halt Dr X and his evil plans.

Together we have saved the world from a truly terrible flood. Let us hope we do not have to deal with Dr X again, but somehow I think that he will be back. Be vigilant!

Thanks and good luck....

Action Man

WANTED

DR X